Grade K

Gifted & Talented™

Reading, Writing & Math

Cover Illustration by Mark Stephens
Written by Tracy Masonis and Larry Martinek, Math Consultant

Spark Publishing

Dear Parents,

Gifted & Talented Reading, Writing & Math has been designed specifically to promote development of analytic thinking, language arts, and math skills. The activities in this book use a variety of critical strategies, including activities to spark your child's imagination, encourage brainstorming, and sharpen math skills.

The activities are intended to help develop reading, writing, and math skills that your child will use at school and home. Most of the activities can be completed directly on the workbook pages. In some instances, though, your child might like to use a separate sheet of paper to interpret what has been read or work out math problems.

While working in this book, your child may be inspired to create his or her own story or math problems. If so, have your child present his or her work and explain the strategies to you. Praise your child's efforts, and encourage him or her to continue creating them. This type of activity not only stimulates creativity and independent thinking, but also deepens your child's love of learning.

© 2007 by Spark Publishing
Adapted from *Gifted & Talented® Reading, Writing & Math Grade K*
© 2003 School Specialty Children's Publishing. Published by Gifted & Talented®, an imprint of School Specialty Children's Publishing, a member of the School Specialty Family.

Flash Kids is a registered trademark of SparkNotes LLC

Spark Publishing
A Division of Barnes & Noble
120 Fifth Avenue
New York, NY 10011
www.sparknotes.com

ISBN-13: 978-1-4114-9558-6
ISBN-10: 1-4114-9558-6

For more information, please visit *www.flashkidsbooks.com*
Please submit changes or report errors to *www.flashkidsbooks.com/errors*

Printed and bound in China

10 9 8 7

Table of Contents—Reading

Groups/Classification

Sequencing

Context Clues

Making Inferences

Predicting Outcomes

Table of Contents—Writing

Print Awareness/Core Sight Words for Writing and Reading

Vocabulary/Labeling

Graphic Organizers for Pre-Writing/Writing

Table of Contents—Math

Numbers and Operations

Patterns

Geometry and Spatial Sense

Measurement

Classification and Data Collection

Number Concepts

The Jungle

Many animals live in the jungle. Find the animals that are small. Which animals are large? Which animals do you think are scaly? Which animals are soft?

Which animal would you want for a pet? Why? Circle your favorite animal above.

Jack, Jill, and Juniper Higgins

Jack, Jill, and Juniper Higgins are all cousins. They even have the same birthday! Jack is very small. Jill is very tall. And Juniper is right in the middle.

In the space between Jack and Jill, draw a picture of Juniper Higgins.

Fast and Slow

Look at the picture below.

 Draw a circle around all of the things that go fast.

 Draw an **X** on each thing that goes slow.

The Tortoise and the Hare

Look at the tortoise and the hare below. Can you name two ways that they are the same?
Can you name two ways that they are different?

I am a hare!

And I am a tortoise!

What would you name the tortoise?
What would you name the hare?

 If the tortoise and the hare were in a race, who do you think would win? Draw a big check mark on your choice.

Basketball!

Coby loves to play basketball. In fact, he has 6 pairs of sneakers just for basketball! Draw a line connecting each pair of matching shoes.

Circle your favorite pair of shoes above.

Thanksgiving Day!

Doug just helped his mom set all of the food on the table for Thanksgiving Day. Which things on the table are hot? Circle all of the hot things with a red crayon. Which things on the table are cold? Circle all of the cold things with a blue crayon.

What kinds of food do you eat on Thanksgiving Day?

Ms. Marilla's Flowers

Ms. Marilla owns a flower shop. She sells only flowers that are purple or pink.

 Circle the flowers that are pink.

 Draw a big check mark by the flowers that are purple.

Fill in the basket by drawing a picture of your favorite flower from Ms. Marilla's shop.

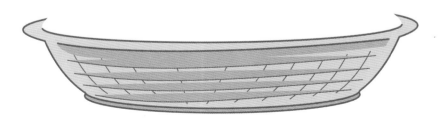

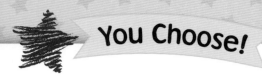
Look at the animals below.

Which animals have feathers?
Which animals have no legs?
Which animals would be fun to ride?

 Circle the animal that would make the best pet for you.

Pete the Peacock!

Look at Pete the Peacock.

Only 1 of the peacocks below is exactly like Pete. Draw a circle around it. What is different about each of the other peacocks?

Lollipop, Lollipops!

There are lots of lollipops in the candy store. In each row below, circle the lollipop that is the same as the one in the jar at the beginning of the row.

Butterfly, Butterflies!

A butterfly is a type of insect. It has 4 wings. Only 2 of the butterflies below look the same. Can you find the 2 matching butterflies? Draw a line to connect them.

Pairs of Parrots!

Look at all the parrots! Only 2 parrots are exactly the same. Can you find them? Circle the pair of parrots that is the same.

What color are their beaks?
Look at their claws.
What color are their tails?

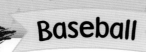

Baseball

Belinda just went to her first baseball game. Many people sat in the bleachers watching it.

Which person is sitting on something soft?
Color that person pink.
Which person is sitting on something hard?
Color that person purple.

Which person is happy?   Which person is short?
Color that person yellow.   Color that person red.
Which person is sad?   Which person is tall?
Color that person blue.   Color that person orange.

Opposites!

Name _____

Look at the pictures below. Draw a line to match each picture to its opposite.

Monkey Business

Look at the pictures below. Draw a line to match each monkey to its opposite.

So Soft!

Which objects below are soft? Color all of the soft things red. Color the rest of the objects in a way that makes sense.

Ziggy and Tiggy

Ziggy the zebra and Tiggy the tiger got lost at the amusement park. Help them find their families.

 Use a black crayon to draw a line connecting everyone in Ziggy's family together. Use an orange crayon to draw a line connecting everyone in Tiggy's family together.

Part of a Group

 Pick 3 pictures that go together in each group. Draw an **X** on the picture that does **not** belong in the group.

Three Things

Circle your answers below.

Which 3 things are on your hand?

   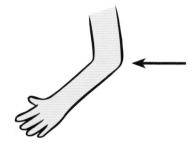

Which 3 things would you need if you were sick?

Which 3 things are in the sky?

Which 3 things would you wear if you were hot?

Creepy Caves!

X ✏️ Many different kinds of animals live in dark caves. Some of the animals pictured below live in caves and some do not. Which animals do not belong? Draw an **X** on the animals that do **not** belong in a cave.

The Ice-Cream Truck

Name _____

Alexander and Jonathan hear the bells on the ice-cream truck. They want to buy an ice-cream cone. The ice-cream truck stops, and they study the ice-cream menu. But something is very strange. There are things on the menu that do not belong. Circle the 3 things that do **not** belong on the menu.

Wrong Purple Things

There are lots of purple things in the picture below. But some of them are not supposed to be purple! Circle the 5 things that should **not** be purple.

What Does Not Belong?

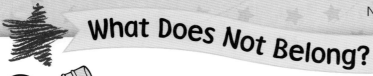

In each row below, use the clue to find the answer. Circle the 1 picture that does **not** begin with the letter **A**.

Circle the 1 picture that does **not** begin with the letter **J**.

Circle the 1 picture that does **not** begin with the letter **S**.

Circle the 1 picture that does **not** begin with the letter **T**.

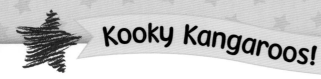

Name _____

Kooky Kangaroos!

Choose 1 of the kangaroos, and explain why it does **not** belong with the others. Then choose another kangaroo and find a new reason why it does **not** belong with the other kangaroos.

Hey, Shorty!

These inchworms were told to line up in order from shortest to longest. But something is wrong. The inchworm that should be first is not where it belongs! Find the inchworm that is out of order and circle it.

Gerry's Giraffes

Gerry lives in Africa. A family of giraffes lives in Gerry's backyard! Each giraffe is a little bit taller than the next giraffe.

 Circle the tallest giraffe.

 Draw a big check mark on the shortest giraffe.

 Draw an **X** on the middle giraffe.

How many spots are on the tallest giraffe?
How tall do you want to be?

The Big Gulp!

Finish the drawing below. Use a pencil or a crayon to connect the dots in order. Can you guess what it is? Start at 1 and end at 10.

Fancy Flower

 Use a pencil to finish the picture so that both sides of the flower look the same. Then color the flower using your favorite colors.

Help Us Get Home!

 Help each animal get home! Use your finger to trace a pathway from left to right. Then draw a line with a pencil or crayon to connect each animal with its home.

The 3 Yellow Kittens

Color the 3 yellow kittens using the clues below.

The first kitten wears silver bracelets and purple boots. It is pushing on the ball of green yarn.

The second kitten wears a red top hat. It is pulling on the ball of green yarn.

The third kitten is lounging on top of the ball of green yarn. It is wearing a blue T-shirt.

The Orchestra

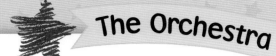

Look at the picture below. Color the 3 violins brown. Color the 4 flutes silver. Color the drums blue. Color the ladies' gowns purple. Color the 2 cellos yellow. Color the rest of the picture in a way that makes sense.

Stop Making Sense!

Look at the picture. A lot of silly things are happening!
Draw a circle around all of the things that do **not** make sense.

Rainbow Clues

Name _____

 Follow the clues below to circle your choices.

Find the object that is **brown** and **hard**.

Find the object that is **yellow** and **long**.

Find the object that is **green** and **sour**.

Find the object that is **blue** and **tiny**.

More Rainbow Clues

 Follow the clues below to circle your choices.

Find the object that is **orange** and **sweet**.

 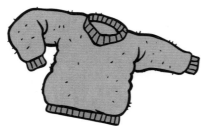  

Find the object that is **yellow** and **hard**.

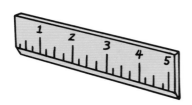   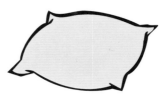

Find the object that is **purple** and **smooth**.

   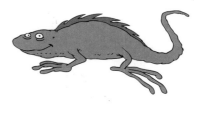

Find the object that is **black** and **sweet**.

Color It In!

Name _____

Color the 1 picture in each row that both words describe.

pink and cold

tall and sad

hot and hard

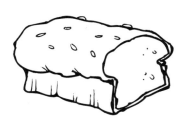   

dirty and soft

Color It In Again!

 Color the 1 picture in each row that both words describe.

round and orange

 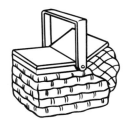  

scared and brown

wet and pointy

large and tired

Yellow Riddles

Find the picture that answers each riddle and color it yellow. Color the other pictures in a way that makes sense.

Hello. Can you guess what's yellow?

I am **yellow** and I keep you **warm**. What am I?

I am **yellow** and **straight**. What am I?

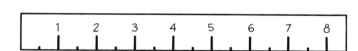

I am **yellow** and **smell good**. What am I?

Grandma Gertie

Grandma Gertie loves flowers. Use the clues below to find the perfect flower for grandma. Circle your answer.

Grandma likes flowers that are pink.
She likes flowers that are tall.
She likes flowers that come with candy.

Jalen's Vacation

Jalen wants to go on vacation. Help him pick out the best spot for his trip.

Jalen does not want to go to a cold place.
Jalen does not want to go to a beach.
Jalen wants to go to a place with games.

 Circle the trip that Jalen should pick.

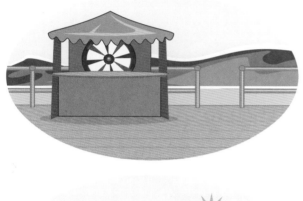

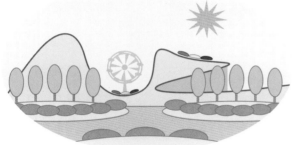

Find the Right Picture

 Which picture goes with the sentence? Draw a big check mark on the correct picture.

> Zelda is playing basketball with her friends by the beach.

Find the Right Picture

Which picture goes with the sentence? Draw a big check mark on the correct picture.

> Miles and Melvin are brothers who love sleeping outside during the summer. One day, they both lie down on a big hammock.

Find the Right Picture

Which picture goes with the sentence? Draw a big check mark on the correct picture.

> Orville and his mother play guitar together.

Which Picture Is Missing?

Look at the pictures on this page. Look at them carefully. Now turn the page.

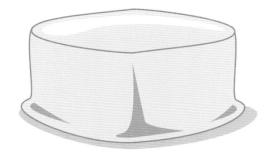

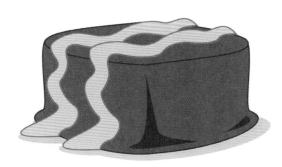

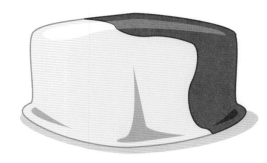

Which Picture Is Missing?

I piece of candy has been eaten. Draw a picture of the missing piece of candy.

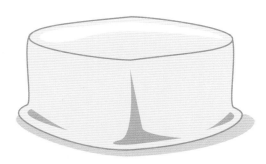

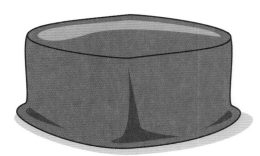

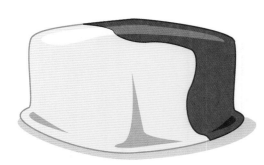

Which Picture Is Missing?

Look at the pictures below. There is a picture missing.

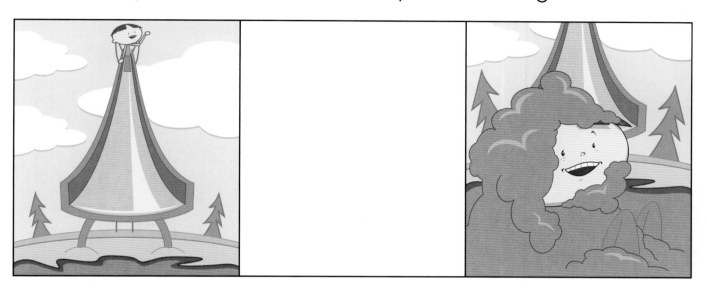

 Draw a big check mark on which one is the missing picture.

Which Picture Is Missing?

Look at the pictures below. There is a picture missing.

 Draw a big check mark on which one is the missing picture.

Which Picture Is Missing?

Look at the pictures below. There is a picture missing.

 Draw a big check mark on which one is the missing picture.

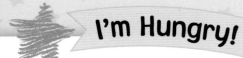

I'm Hungry!

Draw a line to match each food item to the yummy meal it will make.

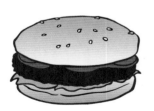

Which Items Do You Not Need?

Nathan is at the barber shop. He is getting his hair cut for the very first time.

 Draw an **X** on the things the barber will **not** need to cut Nathan's hair.

Draw a picture of some other things he might need.

Which Items Do You Not Need?

Lauren and her dad want to play tennis.

 Draw an **X** on the things they do **not** need to play tennis.

 Draw pictures of some other things they might need.

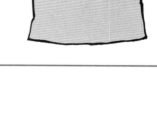

Name _____

Julius and his brother want to help their mother get better. She has a terrible cold.

 Draw an **X** on the things they do **not** need to help her get better.

Draw pictures of some other things Julius and his brother might need.

Which Items Do You Not Need?

Lloyd is working at a bakery.

 Draw an **X** on the things he will **not** need to do his job well.

 Draw pictures of some other things Lloyd might need.

SALT

Model Airplane

Which Picture Is Missing From the Story?

Look at the pictures below. They start to make a story, but the last box is empty.

 Which of these pictures helps to finish the story? Draw a circle around it.

Which Picture Is Missing From the Story?

Look at the pictures below. They start to make a story, but the last box is empty.

 Which of these pictures helps to finish the story? Draw a circle around it.

What Will Happen Next?

Name _____

Look at the picture above.

 Now circle the picture below that shows what happens next.

What Will Happen Next?

Look at the picture above.

 Now circle the picture below that shows what happens next.

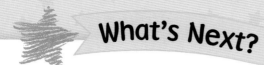

Look at the picture above.

 Now circle the picture below that shows what happens next.

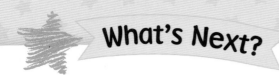

What's Next?

Look at the picture above.

 Now circle the picture below that shows what happens next.

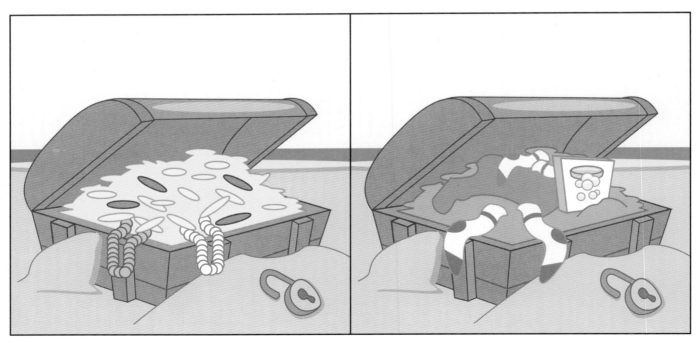

Special Signs

Look at the special signs below. Do you know what they mean?

Draw a line from each word to the box that shows what it means.

Stop

Okay

Quiet

Yes

No

Go

Letters of the Alphabet

These are the letters of the alphabet.
Each letter has a big size and a small size, or upper- and lowercase. Say each letter aloud.

The name of each picture begins with the sound of the letters below it. Say the name of the picture aloud, too.

Oops! A few pictures are missing over the letters. If you come to a letter without a picture, then name something that starts with that letter.

Aa   Bb   Cc   Dd

Ee   Ff   Gg   Hh

Ii   Jj   Kk   Ll

More Letters of the Alphabet

These are the rest of the letters of the alphabet. Each letter has a big size and a small size, or upper- and lowercase. Say each letter aloud.

The name of each picture begins with the sound of the letters below it. Say the name of the picture aloud, too.

Oops! A few pictures are missing over the letters. If you come to a letter without a picture, then name something that starts with that letter.

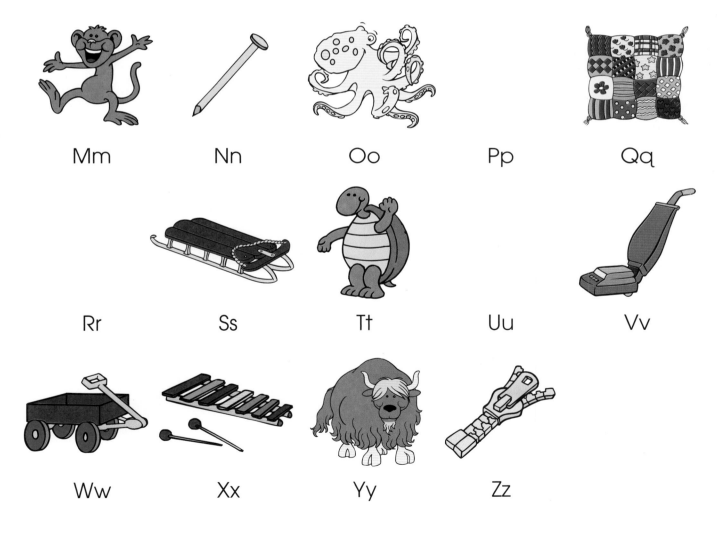

Mm	Nn	Oo	Pp	Qq
Rr	Ss	Tt	Uu	Vv
Ww	Xx	Yy	Zz	

Ask Alice!

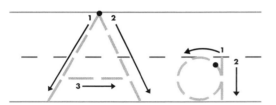 Trace the outline of the letter **A** and **a** below.

Here are some words that start with **A** or **a**. Say them aloud.

after   **Amy**   **ask**   **always**   **Andy**

Read about Alice and circle all the words that start with **A** or **a** you can find.

Always ask Alice for dessert after you eat your dinner. Then she will give you any dessert you ask for!

Write: Ask Alice! _____

Begins With B

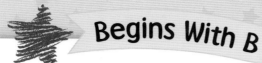

Trace the outline of the letter **B** and **b** below.

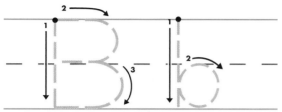

Here are some words that start with **B** or **b**. Say each word aloud.

by   because   been   before   best   both   buy

Do you have a **best** friend?_____

What is the first sound you hear when you say **ball**? What other pictures below begin with the same sound?

 Circle those pictures and say each one aloud.

Tell a story about the picture. Where do you think the three friends are going?

Name _____

 Trace the outline of the letter **C** and **c** below.

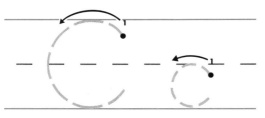

Here are three words that start with **C** or **c**. Can you say them aloud?

 Write each word on the lines below.

cold	call	Could

- - - - - - - - - - - - -

Could you **call** ice cream **cold**?

 Draw a picture of something **cold**.

Whom do you like to **call**?

 Draw a picture.

What **could** happen if you didn't wear a coat in the rain?

 Draw a picture.

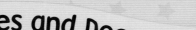
Does and Doesn't!

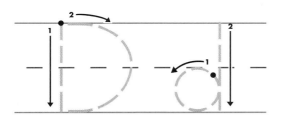

Here are two words that start with **D** or **d**. Say each word aloud and write it on the line below.

Does   **Doesn't**

_____   _____

- -

_____   _____

Look at the picture below. If a picture **does** start with a **D** or **d** sound, then circle it. If it **doesn't** start with **D** or **d**, don't circle it.

Edgar Eats His Eggs Every Day!

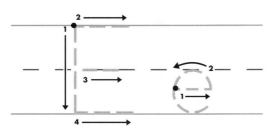

Edgar
eats
eggs
every

Before Edgar eats his eggs every day, he likes to color them.

 Look at the eggs below and color them.

Write the missing **E** or **e** in each word. Then say the whole sentence!

_____dgar _____ats his _____ggs _____very day!

Family Fun!

Name _____

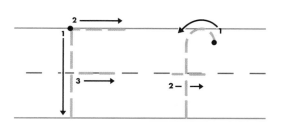

What is the first sound you hear when you say **fun**? What pictures below begin with the same sound?

 Circle those pictures and say each new word aloud.

Here are some more words that start with **F** or **f**. Say each word aloud.

Fly   **from**   **fast**   **First**   **five**   **found**

 Then pick one word to write in a sentence.

_____

Gee, G!

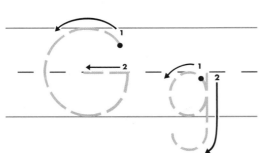

The word **big** ends with the letter **g**. Find the things that end with the letter **g**. One is done for you.

Find 9 more things and circle them.

Here are some words that start with **G** or **g**. Say each word aloud.

 Then pick one word to write in a sentence.

give   **Giving**   **gave**   **Go**   **green**

_____

Name _____

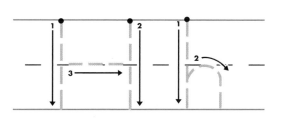

Look at the hare in the box below. What other pictures on the page begin with the same sound?

 Circle those pictures and say each word aloud.

Here are some words that start with **H** or **h**. Say each word aloud.

Here   **happy**   **Hello**

Write a sentence about the hare. _____

_____

Name _____

  Trace the letters below for practice.

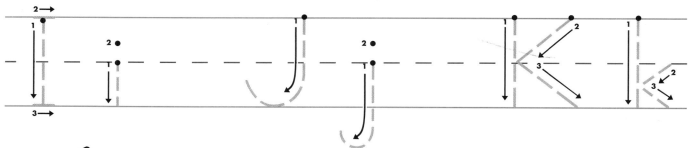

Read the words and sentences below. Then write each word on the line.

Its   **Its** name is Alfred.

_____

Just a minute, please.

Just   **Just** a minute, please.

_____

know   I **know** how to read.

_____

Laughing Lizards!

live on the lines below.

_____ live _____

 Circle the pictures below that start with the same sound as **lizard**.

One day, my mom and I went for a walk. "Did you hear that?" I asked.

"Hear what?" asked Mom.

"That!" Then we both heard somebody laughing.

"Who is laughing so hard?" asked my mom.

We looked around, but there was no one there. Suddenly, something moved. It was a lizard with sunglasses on! He was laughing so hard his tail was flopping from side to side.

"Why, you're the happiest lizard I've ever seen!" said my mom.

"**Let** him **live** with us, please, Mom?" I asked.

"Of course, laughing lizards are lucky!" she said.

 **Magic Middles!**

Look at the picture in the middle of the page. What is it? Name all the pictures on the page.

Then color the pictures **red** that start with the same sound as the picture in the middle of the page.

More **M** or **m** words:

May   **made**   **many**

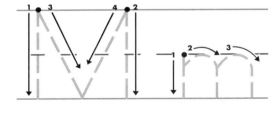

Say each word aloud.

 Then write each word below on the lines.

May   **May** I go to the bathroom?   _____

made   That was **made** by me.   _____

many   I have **many** friends.   _____

The Missing N!

Each person is missing something that begins with the letter **N** or **n**. Read the sentences aloud.

Then draw a napkin for the girl. Draw a nest for the bird. Write a name for the woman. Draw a needle for the grandma.

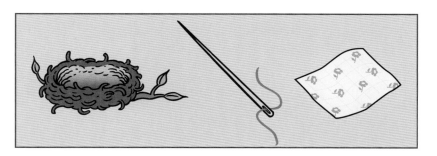

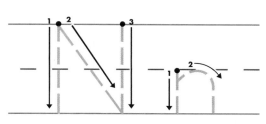

Now I need a napkin!

I have **no** name! _____

Something is **not** right!

Where is my **needle**?

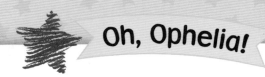

Oh, Ophelia!

Once there was an **old** lady named Ophelia who flew **over** the mountains, **off** a cliff, and **over** the **open** sea — all **on** her bicycle! It's true! Ophelia attached wings and a motor to her bike, and **off** she went! It is said that sometimes you can even see Ophelia peddling her bike *right past the moon!*

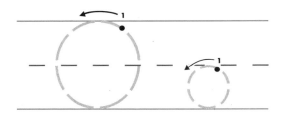

Word Box		
Once	old	over
off	on	open

Say the words in the word box aloud.

Write a sentence (or two!) about Ophelia. Use one of the words in the word box in your sentence.

Bonus! Use three words from the **Word Box** in a sentence or story.

_____

_____

Put-Pull

Pam put the **plums** in a wagon and tried to **pull** them up the hill.

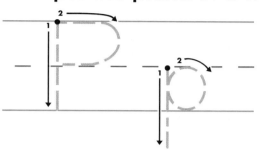

Say these words aloud. Then write each word on the line.

Pam _____

put _____

plums _____

pull _____

Write a sentence using two of these words. Say your sentence aloud. Then draw a picture about what you **pulled**.

_____

_____

_____

Queen Quackers!

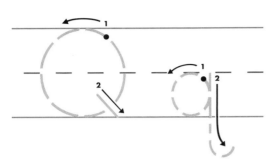

One day, the **queen's** huge palace was filled to the highest tower with popcorn! Her cook had popped too many kernels. **"Queen Quackers! Queen Quackers!"** her servants called. (Every room and every tower was filled with popcorn.) "We have to get you out of here!"

"Don't be silly! I will just eat my way out!" And she did for an entire year!

Write a sentence about Queen Quackers. Then draw a picture of what happened to the queen.

_____

_____

_____

_____

_____

Race Car R!

R and **r** are hidden in the picture below. Look carefully to find 6 of them. Then circle them!

Here are some words that start with **R** or **r**. Read the words aloud.

Ready   **round**   **read**   **right**

 Then write a sentence using one of the words._____

_____

Same Sounds

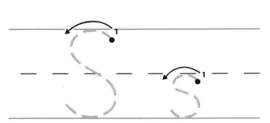

Say the names of the pictures in each row.

 Circle the pictures that begin with the same sound.

 Then draw a new picture that begins with that sound.

Here are some more words that begin with **S** or **s**. Say each word aloud.

Word Box				
some	Stop	sing	sit	sleep

Toy Box

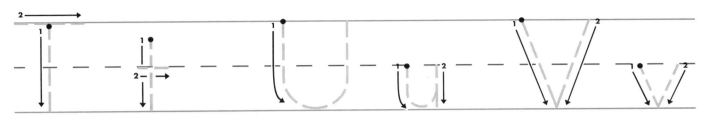

Toy Box

Here is a toy box filled with lots of **Tt, Uu,** and **Vv** words. Think of some toys whose names start with these letters and that could be inside the toy box!

 Write down your ideas.

_____

_____

Wonderful W

Name _____

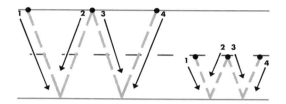

All the pictures on this page begin with the letter **W** or **w**.

Find something in the bathroom. What is it?

Find something that is clear. What is it?

Find something that changes all the time. What is it?

Find something that you can get water from. What is it?

Find something that is part of a bird. What is it?

 Draw a line from the question to the picture you choose.

walk	When	which	wish	would
were	wash	why	What	write

When do you **walk** to school?

 _____ Write a sentence using one of these words.

_____

What would you **wish** for from a fairy?

 _____ Draw a picture of your answer.

 _____ Use **wash** in a sentence. _____

_____

 _____ Use **why** in a sentence. _____

_____

 _____ Use **write** in a sentence.

_____

 _____ Use **were** in a sentence. _____

_____

Letters and Lines Xx, Yy, Zz

 Color the **X** and **x** blue.

 Color the **Y** and **y** red.

 Color the **Z** and **z** green.

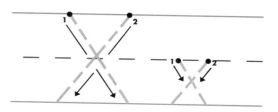

| X x | Y y | Z z |

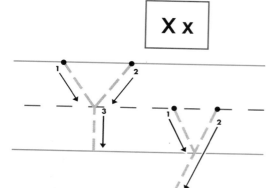

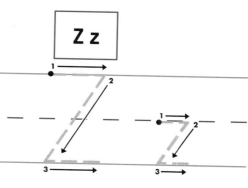

Do you know how to use a **yoyo**? _____

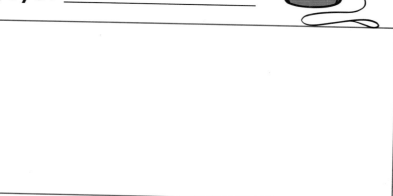

Draw a picture of yourself doing a trick with a yoyo.

What is your favorite zoo animal?

 Draw a picture of it.

 Draw a line from each letter to the one that will look the same when the missing parts are filled in.

 Finish the missing parts. One is done for you.

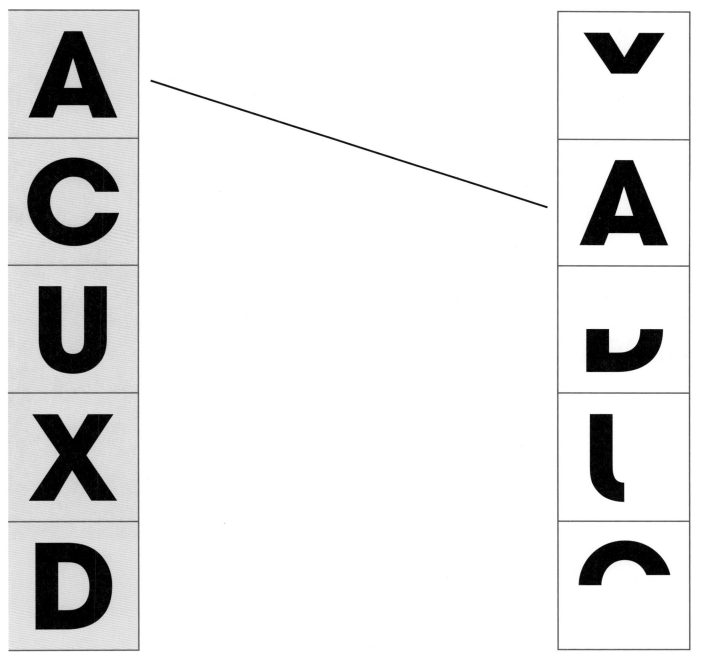

Missing Letters!

Look at the alphabet patterns of big and small letters.

 Write the missing letters.

A B c d E F g ____

I J ____ ____ M ____

o p ____ ____ s ____ U ____ w x Y ____

A b C d

E f ____ h ____ j ____ I M n O p

____ r ____ t U v ____ x ____ z

a b C D e f G H

i j ____ ____ m n ____ ____

q r S T ____ ____ ____ W X y z

 **Vowel Riddles**

Read each animal riddle.

 Write the missing vowels to finish the words. Vowels are **a, e, i, o, u,** and sometimes **y**.

 Draw a line to the animal that solves each riddle.

I like the w _____ ter.

I am a b _____ rd.

I h _____ p.

I am s _____ ft.

I like to eat b _____ n _____ n _____ s.

I like to swing in tr _____ _____ s.

I live in the w _____ ter.

I am scal _____ .

I like to eat p _____ anuts.

I am big and gra _____ .

Matching Sounds

Say the names of the pictures in each row.

 Circle the pictures that begin with the same sound.

 Then draw a new picture that begins with that sound.

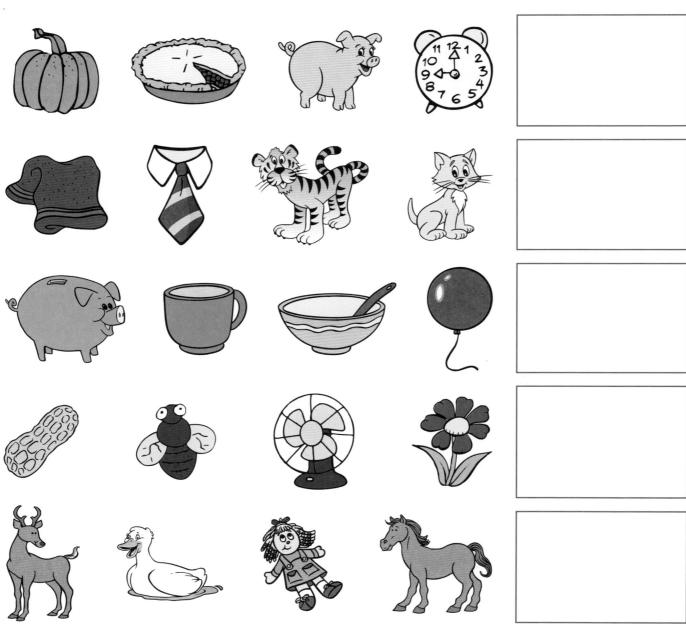

Hidden Animals!

Look at each animal below. Look at each animal's name.

 Color the letter boxes that spell each animal's name.

turtle

S	T	R	T	E	L	U

seal

E	A	T	Y	L	S	Z

dog

G	D	E	O	P	Q	I

gerbil

B	L	R	K	G	E	I

tiger

R	G	L	F	T	I	E

cat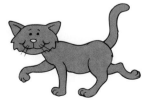

H	S	W	T	P	C	A

Your Very Own Letter!

What letter does your name begin with?

 Write that letter in the box below. Make it as big as you can.

 Draw a colorful design in the space around the letter.

Can you think of some words that begin with the same letter as your name?

 Write them on the line below.

_____

For fun: Cut out pictures that begin with "your" letter and glue them on to a sheet of paper. Then write what each new picture is below it.

Name _____

Draw a line from each word to the box that is the same shape as the word. The first one is done for you.

 1. camel ———————

 2. cake

 3. zipper

 4. rocket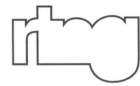

 5. rake

 6. ring

More Words!

Draw a line from each word to the box that is the same shape as the word. The first one is done for you.

1. flower ———————

2. violin

3. lamp

4. spider

5. wagon

6. leaf

Word Shapes

Copy each word into the box that is the same shape as the word. Then draw a line to match the word to its picture. The first one is done for you.

| moon   apple   jeep   gorilla |
| basket   toaster   bugle |

1. **moon**

2. apple

3. jeep

4. gorilla

5. basket

6. toaster

7. bugle

This Way and That Way

Look at the pictures and words below.

 Write the missing letters to make word pairs.

Hint: The second word is the first word spelled backwards.

gum   M ____ ____

stop   P ____ ____ ____

pets   S ____ ____ ____

net   **10**   T ____ ____

BONUS:

Palindromes!

Palindromes are words or sentences whose letters read the same forward **and** backwards! The words below are palindromes. Say them aloud.

noon	Pop	bib	Bob	Anna
pup	Hannah	Mom	Dad	

 Write a sentence with a palindrome in it.

_____

Secret Word

Find the secret word.
Read all the clues.

 Then write each
letter in the correct nut.

S is on top.
L is on the bottom.
Q is under S.
U is the third letter.
R is on top of R.
I is the fourth letter.
E is on top of L.
R is on top of E.

I feel
nutty!

What word did you spell? Write it on the line.

_____

Tell a story about the picture. What do you think will happen to all
those nuts?

Name _____

Find the letter that is missing from each group of words.

 Then write the letters in the spaces and solve the riddle.

What has four legs and can't walk?

A ____ ____ ____ ____ ____ !

_OP
PO_
WI_H
_HANK YOU

The missing
letter is ____.

C_T
B_T
_PPLE
_ND

The missing
letter is ____.

_EAR
_ILL
CU_
_ANK

The missing
letter is ____.

_OVE
A__
_AMP
APP_E

The missing
letter is ____.

_GG
H_LP
H_ART
_ND

The missing
letter is ____.

Hidden Words

Look at the words in the box.

Find them in the puzzle and circle them. Two are done for you.

out	pack	sock	pick
move	cute	thank	

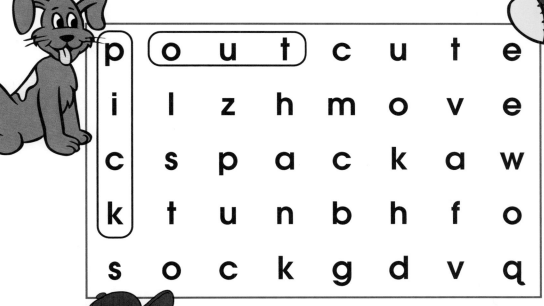

p	o	u	t	c	u	t	e
i	l	z	h	m	o	v	e
c	s	p	a	c	k	a	w
k	t	u	n	b	h	f	o
s	o	c	k	g	d	v	q

The Sneaker Speaks!

Look at all the parts of a sneaker:

I am so tired of people always mixing up the proper names of my parts. It makes me want to step on somebody!

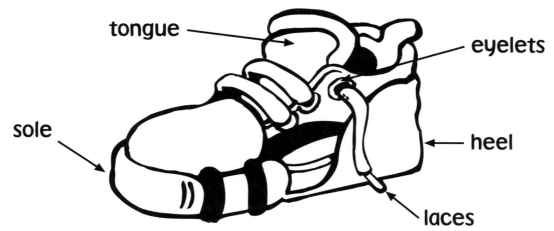

tongue

eyelets

sole

heel

laces

 Now write the parts on this sneaker.

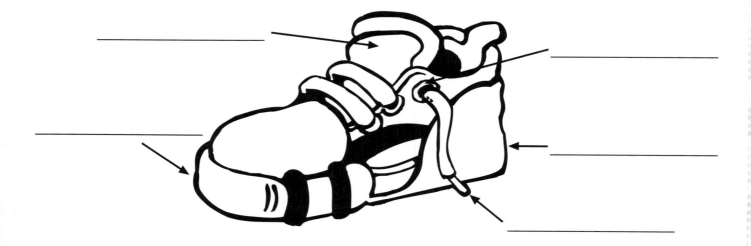

Make up a story about the sneaker. Why is he or she upset?

Name _____

Heather is working hard to stay healthy.

I love to exercise. It is so good for my body.

shoulders

arms

stomach

back

legs

calves

 Now label the parts of her body.

Do you like to run, jog, or maybe even jump rope?

 Write what kind of exercise you like to do.

_____

Timber!

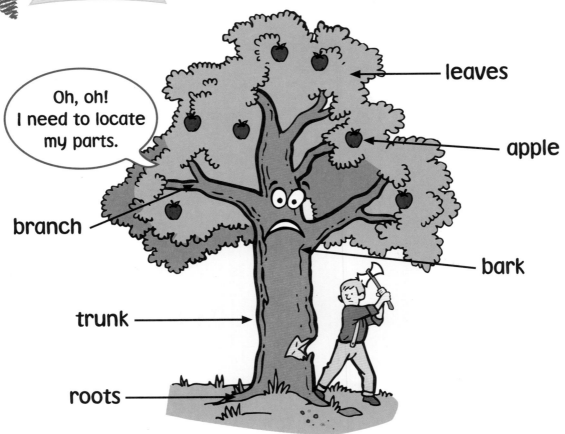

Oh, oh! I need to locate my parts.

leaves

apple

branch

bark

trunk

roots

Say the names aloud of the parts of the tree.

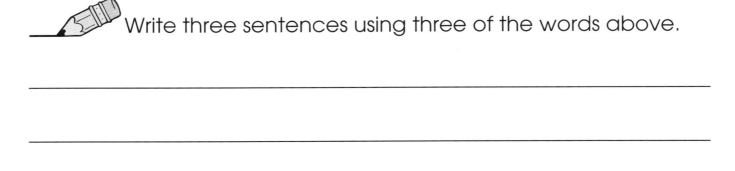

Write three sentences using three of the words above.

_____

_____

_____

Write the name of your favorite fruit on the line below.

_____

Princess Pictures

 Circle what this picture is about.

a nurse   a princess   a witch

 Write a sentence about the

picture. _____

_____

_____

 Circle what the princess is doing.

juggling   singing   talking

 Write a sentence about the

picture. _____

_____

_____

 What is your favorite flavor of ice cream?

_____

Clever Coyotes!

Name _____

What animals are pictured here?

 Circle your answer.

cows   coyotes   cats

 Write a sentence or sentences about the picture.

_____

_____

Sentences: Complete Thoughts

A sentence has a **beginning** and an **ending**. A sentence tells a **complete thought**. When you write a sentence, make sure it is **all** there! Just a beginning or just an ending is not a complete sentence!

Draw a line from each sentence's beginning to its **correct** ending so each one makes sense.

I play   sings.

My mom   tennis.

Your dog   collect shells.

She likes to   howls.

Punctuation: Periods

Use a **period** to end a **complete sentence**.
A period is like a stop sign!

I love to sing.

My dog runs a lot.

 Add periods at the end of each sentence.

My cat is orange and black____

A bird caught a worm____

My room is messy____

The baby bunny was soft____

My brother is silly____

Rules of Capitalization

1. The **first word** of a sentence always begins with a capital letter.

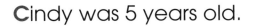

The rain was cold.

 Now you write a sentence. _____

_____

2. **People's names** always begin with a capital letter.

Cindy was 5 years old.

 Write a sentence with a **name** in it. _____

_____

 Read the sentences below and circle the words that need a capital letter.

 Then write each sentence correctly.

eddie and max are twins.

_____

my teacher is very tall.

_____

More Capital Rules

3. The name of a **place** always begins with a capital letter.

Florida is very hot and sunny.

 Write the name of a **place**. _____

4. The names of **months** always begin with a capital letter.

My baby brother was born in **A**ugust.

Write the name of a **month**. _____

Read the sentences below and circle the words that need a capital letter.

Then write each sentence correctly.

In july we go to the beach.

_____

texas is a large state.

_____

in april we go to spain with Uncle bob for one week.

_____

A New Pet!

Name _____

Aunt FiFi just gave Gabriella a new poodle. Gabriella has no idea what she will need to take care of her new pet! Help brainstorm some ideas for Gabriella.

 Circle the words that tell Gabriella what she will need.

Then write some of your own.

dog food

strawberry
ice cream

leash

lipstick

dog brush

laundry
detergent

_____

_____

_____

 Do you think Gabriella will like her new pet? Why or why not?

_____

Happy Hearts!

Look at the heart in the middle of the page. Inside it says, "Things I Care About." Attached to it are 6 little hearts.

Inside the little hearts draw a picture or write 6 things that you care about.

Things I Care About

Tell a story about one thing you wrote or colored inside a heart.

The World's Best Birthday Party!

Look at the birthday cake in the middle of the page.

 On each candle write or draw one thing you would need to have a great birthday party. The first one is done for you.

School Shopping List

Sasha and her mom are at the school supply store.

 Circle what Sasha and her mom should buy for school.

Say aloud what **you** would choose to buy for school.

Draw a picture and write the word that tells what you would want most for school.

_____

Rhyme Time!

Rhyming words are words whose **endings** sound the same, like **cat** and **hat**.

Draw a line to match each pair of rhyming words to its picture.

moon-spoon

punk-skunk

weird-beard

"Hey, this isn't cheese!"

snake-cake

Putting It Together

Think of two words that rhyme and go together to make a silly picture.

Write the words and draw the picture.

This is a _____ - _____.

Here are some words to help you. Try to think of more on your own.

think   toe   drink   sleet

grow   wink   Joe   glow

feet   snow   meat   dough

stink   pink   treat   beet

Words Come Alive!

It's fun to draw words and make them look like what they mean.

 Choose one of the words below and draw it.

sad	love	silly	candy
happy	cold	ugly	scaly

Character!

A **character** is a person in a story.

Before you write a story you want to think about:

Who will be in your story?

Answer the questions below to help you **brainstorm** a character that you want to write about.

Let's Go!

Will your character be a boy or a girl, a man or a woman?

 Circle your choice.

 How old will your character be?

_____

What will your character look like? Ugly? Scary? Pretty? Strong? Clean?

 Circle your choice.

Character!

How tall will your character be?

 Write your choice.

_____

Will your character be fat or skinny or in the middle?

 Circle your choice.

What color hair will your character have? Or will he or she be bald?

 Write your choice. _____

Will your character have wavy hair or straight hair? Long or short hair?

 Circle your choice.

What shape of face will your character have? Round, oval, square, heart-shaped?

 Circle your choice.

What color eyes will your character have? Blue? Green? Brown? Two different colors?

 Circle your choice.

 Character!

What kind of nose will your character have?
A long pointy nose? A big nose? A tiny little nose?

 Circle your choice.

What will your character's teeth look like? Will they be shiny and white? Yellow and broken? Is your character missing teeth?

 Circle your choice.

How will your character smell?
Like sweet perfume? Sweaty? Stinky?

 Circle your choice.

 What do you want to name your character?

_____

Hello, I am Esmerelda-Penelope-Pineapple-McGilacutty!

Name _____

Draw a picture of your character.

Write a story about something that happens to your character on the lines below.

_____

_____

_____

_____

_____

_____

Think of a new thing you can make by making something **larger**.
Three are done for you.

Toothpick	into	a javelin
Table knife	into	a saw
Coffee cup	into	a swimming pool

Make it larger and change a…

_____ into _____

_____ into _____

_____ into _____

Now draw a picture of something you can change by making it **larger**.

Before   into   **After**

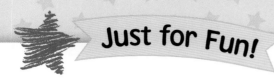

Just for Fun!

List the things you can make by making them **smaller**. Three are done for you.

Helicopter	into	a fan
Couch	into	a foot rest
Swimming pool	into	a birdbath

Make it smaller and change a…

_____ into _____

_____ into _____

_____ into _____

Now draw a picture of something you can change by making it **smaller**.

Before into **After**

Drivers Wanted!

Draw a line to connect each person with his or her vehicle.

Simple Shadows

 Draw a line to connect each object with its shadow.

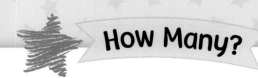

How Many?

 Circle the two numbers that add up to exactly 10.

9   3   4   1   5   2

 Circle the two numbers that add up to exactly 10.

9   3   4   7   5   2

 Circle the two numbers that add up to exactly 20.

10   3   14   19   5   10

 Circle the two numbers that add up to exactly 20.

19   5   14   17   6   2

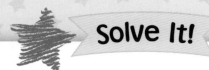

Solve It!

Billy is 5 years old. His mother is 30 years old. How old will Billy be when his mother is 33 years old?

 Circle your answer.

5   6   7   8   9   10

Nick and Christy shared a box of cookies. They ate half of the cookies at lunch. Then they ate half of what they had left at dinnertime. Nick and Christy then had 3 cookies left. How many cookies did they start with?

 Circle your answer.

7   8   9   10   11   12   13

Uh, Oh, I Forgot!

All of the three children below have forgotten to put on something in the morning!

 Draw a line to connect the children with the piece of clothing they are missing.

We Go Together!

 Circle the three numbers that add up to exactly 12.

9   3   4   1   5   2

 Circle the three numbers that add up to exactly 20.

9   8   4   7   5   2

 Circle the three numbers that add up to exactly 30.

10   1   15   19   5   10

 Circle the four numbers that add up to exactly 100.

20   30   25   25   30   20

60 Seconds!

Read the questions below. Then circle your answers.

✏️ JoJo lives close to his school. He walks from home to school in 90 seconds. Does it take him more than 2 minutes or less than 2 minutes to get to school?

more than 2 minutes   less than 2 minutes

✏️ How long does it take JoJo to walk to school and then walk back home again?

I minute   2 minutes   3 minutes

✏️ Louisa is 40 inches tall. Is she more than 4 feet tall or less than 4 feet tall?

more than 4 feet   less than 4 feet

✏️ How much taller or shorter than 4 feet is she?

0   4   8   12   16 inches

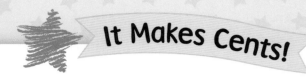

It Makes Cents!

If you put a dime in the gumball machine, you will get three pieces of gum.

How many pieces of gum will you get for 30 cents?

 Circle your answer.

0   3   6   9   12

How much will a dozen pieces of gum cost?

 Circle your answer.

20¢   40¢   60¢   80¢   100¢

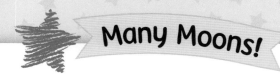
Many Moons!

Look at the picture below. Are there more stars or more moons?

 Circle your answer.   stars   moons

How many more?

 Circle your answer.   1   2   3   4   5

In the picture above, are there more planets or more moons?

 Circle your answer.   moons   planets

How many more?

 Circle your answer.   1   2   3   4   5

How many total objects are in the picture?

 Circle your answer.   10   15   20   25   30

How Many?

Name _____

Read the questions below. Then circle your answers.

 How many legs do 3 dogs have altogether?

0   4   8   12   16

 If you counted 20 legs total, how many dogs would there be?

1   2   3   4   5

 How many legs do 2 birds have altogether?

0   2   4   5   6

 If you counted 6 legs total, how many birds would there be?

1   2   3   4   5

How Many Again?

How many rows of cars are shown in the picture?

 Circle your answer.   1   2   3   4   5

How many rows of tulips are there in Mrs. Martin's garden?

 Circle your answer.   0   3   5   7   9

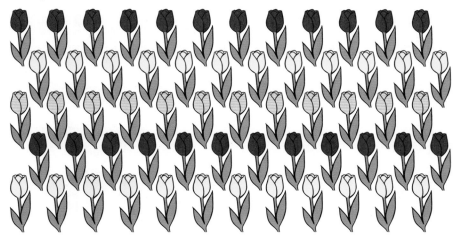

Each chocolate bar has 6 pieces. How many pieces are there altogether in 3 candy bars?

 Circle your answer.

0   6   12   18   24

Name _____

How many coins are there
in the picture?

 Circle your answer.

10   15   20   25   30

Mrs. Magill's class has 10 students. Mrs. Magee's
class has 10 students, and Mrs. MacDonald's class
has 10 students. How many groups of 5 can be
made out of the students in these 3 classes?

 Circle your answer.

5   6   7   8   9

Nothing to It!

Katie had 15 cents to spend at the county fair. She bought a balloon for 5 cents and an ice-cream cone for 10 cents. How much money did Katie have left at the end of the day?

 Circle your answer.   0   1   2   3   4   5

If you have two dimes, how many more dimes do you need to have a total of 20 cents?

 Circle your answer.

0   1   2   3   4   5

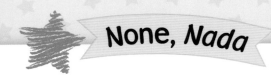

Name _____

None, Nada

Billy's mom gave him 5 dollars to play video games at the arcade. At the end of the day, Billy had no money left. How many dollars did he spend at the arcade?

 Circle your answer.　0　1　2　3　4　5

Ten take away what number equals ten?

 Circle your answer.　0　1　2　3　4　5

 10 - ??? = 10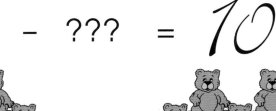

Wholes and Parts

 Color half of each of the following pictures. Use a different color for each one. Be creative!

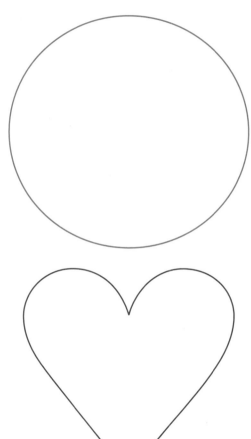

Which one would you rather have: one piece of a candy bar cut into 3 parts or two pieces of a candy bar cut into 10 parts?

Circle your answer.

1 piece of 3   2 pieces of 10

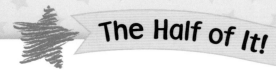
Mom cut a pie into 12 pieces. Then her children ate half ($\frac{1}{2}$) of the pie for dessert. How many pieces were left?

 Circle your answer.

0 1 2 3 4 5 6 7 8

Color only half of the circles in each row below. Use a different color for each one.

◯ ◯ ◯ ◯ ◯ ◯ ◯ ◯ ◯ ◯

How many circles are **not** colored?

Circle your answer. 0 1 2 3 4 5 6

◯◯◯◯◯◯◯◯◯◯◯◯◯◯◯◯◯◯◯◯

How many circles are **not** colored?

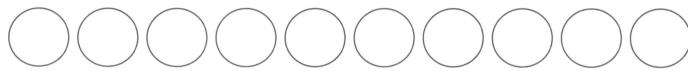 Circle your answer. 5 6 7 8 9 10 11 12

◯ ◯ ◯ ◯ ◯ ◯ ◯ ◯ ◯

How many circles are **not** colored?

 Circle your answer. 2 2$\frac{1}{2}$ 3 3$\frac{1}{2}$ 4 4$\frac{1}{2}$ 5

Rainy Day Schedule

When the children got to school, they lined up their rainboots in a straight line outside of the classroom door. How many rainboots were there altogether?

 Circle your answer.   10   12   14   16   18

How many children are in the classroom?

 Circle your answer.   6   7   8   9   10

Then some of the children went home early. They took their rainboots with them when they left. How many children went home?

 Circle your answer.   2   3   4   5   6

Submarine Subway

A submarine had 5 sea horse passengers.
At the first stop, 5 sea horses got on and 1 sea horse got off.
At the next stop, 6 sea horses got on and 0 sea horses got off.
How many sea horses are on the submarine now?

 Circle your answer.   10   11   12   13   14   15

Then the submarine picked up 5 passengers.
At the next stop, 5 sea horses got on and 7 sea horses got off.
At the next stop, 2 sea horses got on and 8 sea horses got off.
How many sea horses are on the submarine now?

 Circle your answer.   10   11   12   13   14   15

Clap Your Hands!

Name _____

Clap your hands once, pat the top of your head two times, clap your hands three times, and then pause. Repeat this pattern three times.

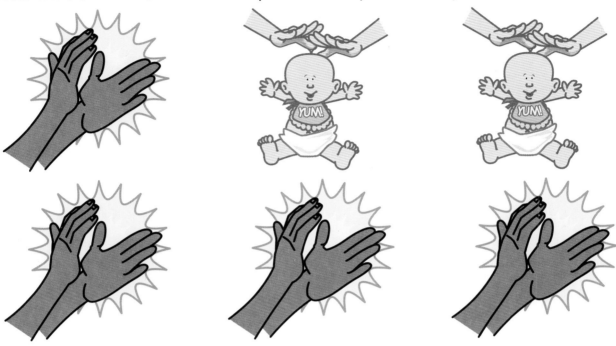

Clap your hands and pat your head as shown in the picture below.

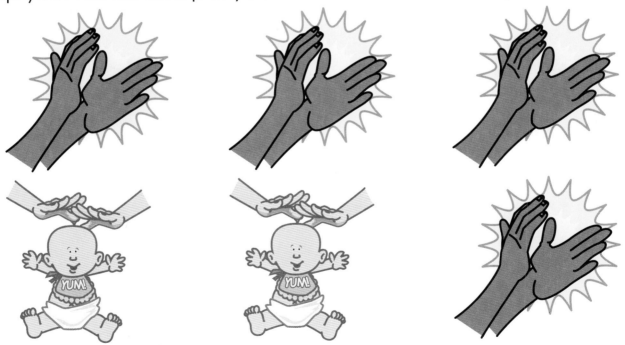

Perfect Patterns

Use a crayon or a pencil to make a copy of this pattern.

_____

Copy the pattern above backwards.

_____

Now design a pattern of your own!

_____

Copy your pattern backwards.

_____

More Perfect Patterns!

Use a crayon or a pencil to make a copy of this pattern.

_____

 Copy the pattern above backwards.

_____

 Now design a pattern of your own!

_____

 Copy your pattern backwards.

_____

Penelope and Her Patterns

Penelope loves patterns! She dreams about them all day long.

 Use a crayon or a pencil to help Penelope finish each of the following patterns by drawing what comes next.

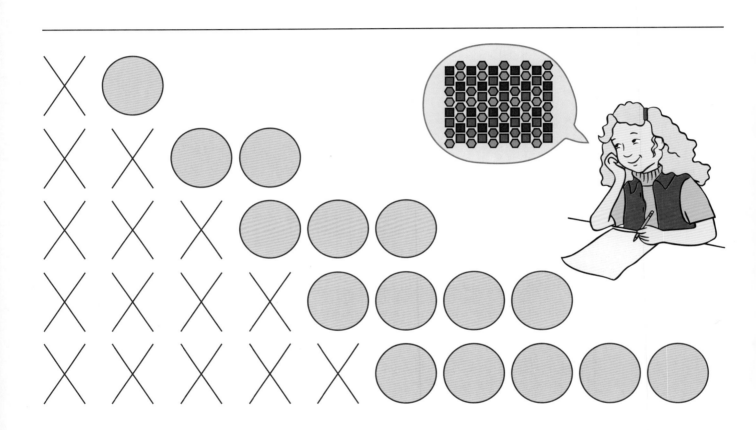

The Toy Box! Inside, Above, Behind, Beside

 Circle the object that is **inside** the toy box.

 Draw a square around the object that is **above** the toy box.

 Draw a triangle around the object that is **behind** the toy box.

Draw a diamond around the object that is **beside** the toy box.

Monster Mash!

Oh no! A three-ton monster came along and sat on each of the shapes below.

✏️ Draw a line to match each shape before and after the monster sat on them.

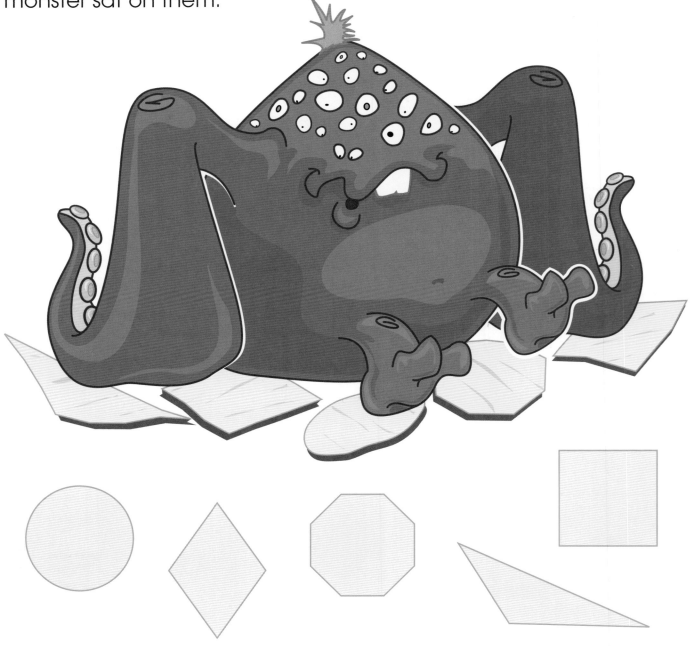

Copy Cat!

Use your crayons to make a copy of this design.

More Copy Cat!

 Use your crayons to make a copy of this design.

Up and Down—Left and Right

Vertical lines go up and down, like the vertebra in your spine.

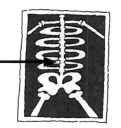

Horizontal lines go left to right, like the horizon at sunset.

 Circle the pictures below that show things that are **vertical**.

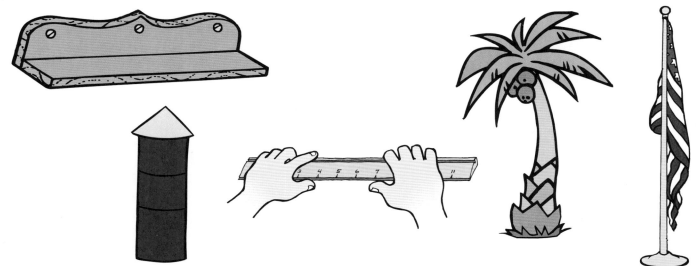

 Circle the pictures below that show things that are **horizontal**.

Up and Down—Left and Right

Draw and color a picture of something that is **vertical**.

Draw and color a picture of something that is **horizontal**.

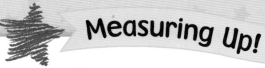

Circle the word that tells how much something **weighs**.

ounce   foot   quart

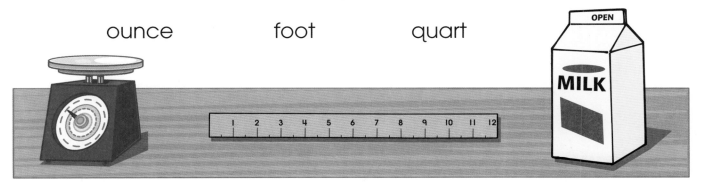

Circle the word that tells how **long** something is.

ton   inch   gallon

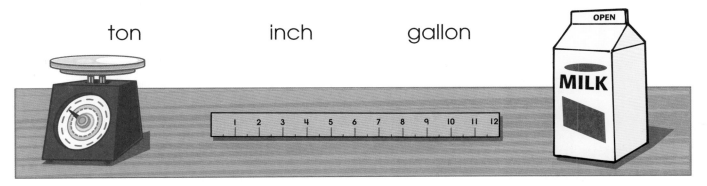

 Circle the word that tells how much something **holds**.

pound   foot   quart

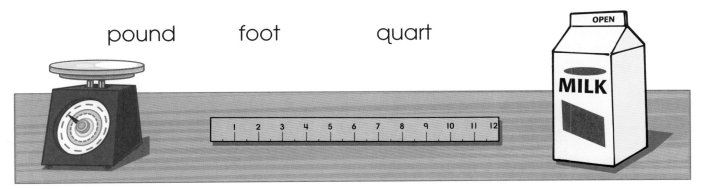

Measuring Machines

Circle what you would use to measure the **weight** of a dog.

Circle what you would use to measure the **amount** of orange juice left in the glass.

Circle what you would use to measure the **distance** around a pumpkin.

Full or Empty?

Circle each picture that shows something is **full**.

Draw a square around each picture that shows something
is **empty**.

Full or Empty?

Name _____

 Circle the picture above that shows a **full** gas tank.

Draw a square around the picture above that shows an **empty** gas tank.

Draw and color a picture of something that is **full**.

Draw and color a picture of something that is **empty**.

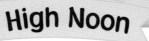

High Noon

 Circle the things you usually do **before** lunch.

 Circle the things you usually do **after** lunch.

Kinds of Measurement

Do you measure your **age** in years or in miles?

 Circle your answer.   years   miles

Do you measure your **height** in quarts or in inches?

 Circle your answer.   quarts   inches

Do you measure your **weight** in weeks or in pounds?

 Circle your answer.   weeks   pounds

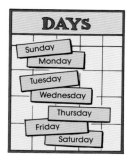

Smallest and Largest

 Circle the **shortest**.

 a foot an inch  a mile

 Draw a square around the **longest**.

a foot an inch a mile

 Circle the **shortest**.

 a year an hour  a day

 Draw a square around the **longest**.

 a year an hour a day

 Circle the **lightest**.

 a ton a pound  an ounce

 Draw a square around the **heaviest**.

 a ton a pound  an ounce

Match Maker

Draw a line to connect objects that do the same kind of thing.

Name _____

Draw a line to connect objects that do the same kind of thing.

The Same But Different!

How are an ice cube and a basketball **similar** to each other?

 Circle your answer.   both are square   neither are flat

How are an ice cube and a basketball **different** from each other?

 Circle your answer.

both are flat   one is square and one is not

How are a square and a cube **similar**?

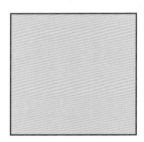 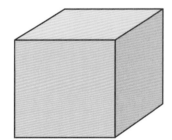

 Circle your answer.   both are square   both are round

How are a square and a cube **different** from each other?

 Circle your answer.

both are flat   one is flat and one is not

Come Together

Look at the objects below.

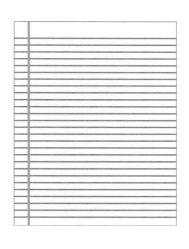

Which objects go together?

_____ Draw a line to connect the two objects that belong together.

The Same But Different!

 Draw a line to connect two objects that have something in common.

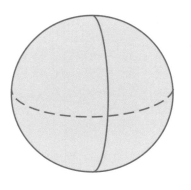

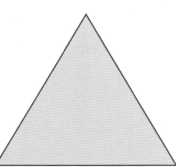

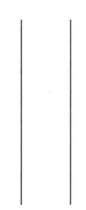

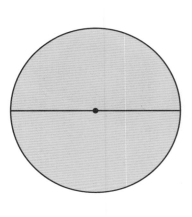

Draw and color two things that go together.

Name _____

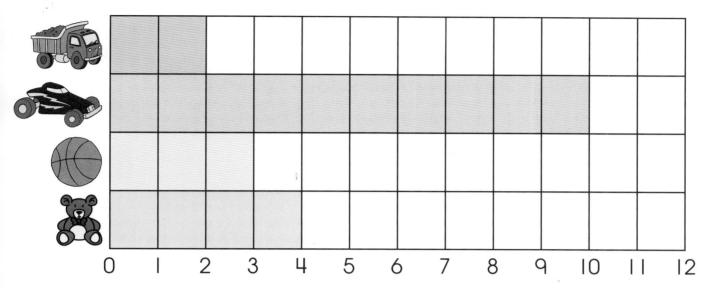

John made a chart of some of his toys.

Which toy does he have the **most** of?

 Circle your answer.

dump trucks   cars   bears   basketballs

Which toy does he have the **least** of?

 Circle your answer.

dump trucks   cars   bears   basketballs

How many more bears than basketballs does John have?

 Circle your answer.   0   1   2   3   4   5

Graph It Again!

Name _____

Billy made a chart of all of his money.

Which coin does he have the **most** of?

 Circle your answer.   pennies   nickels   dimes   quarters

Which coin does she have the **least** of?

 Circle your answer.   pennies   nickels   dimes   quarters

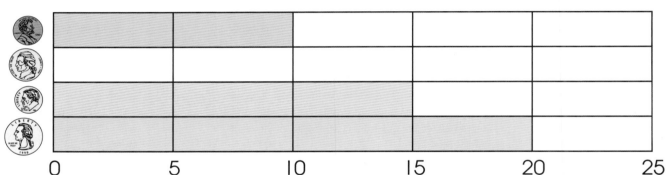

Now try this! Take 20 pennies and drop them on the floor. Count how many heads and tails are showing.

 Fill in the bar graph.

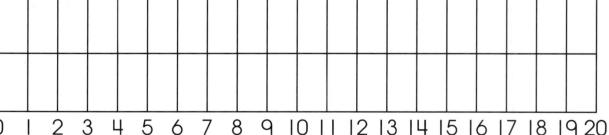

Repeat this three more times and see how the numbers change.

Half Full or Half Empty?

This cup is half full. It contains
8 ounces of juice. How much
does the cup hold when it is full?

 Circle your answer.   0   8   14   16   18   20

This pitcher holds 13 ounces of water. Half of the water has been
poured out. How many ounces are left?

Circle your answer.   5 $5\frac{1}{2}$ 6 $6\frac{1}{2}$ 7 $7\frac{1}{2}$ 8

The Half of It!

This cup is full and contains 24 ounces of juice. After William drinks half of the juice, how many ounces will be left?

 Circle your answer.   10   11   12   13   14   23

This pitcher is half full and contains $3\frac{1}{2}$ ounces of water. How much does the pitcher hold when it is full?

 Circle your answer.   5 $5\frac{1}{2}$ 6 $6\frac{1}{2}$ 7

Jada's Pets

Jada and her friends decided they would make clothes for Jada's pets. Jada has 2 dogs, 1 cat, and 1 bird.

How many shoes should the girls make for all of the animals?

 Circle your answer.

8   10   12   14   16

How many hats should the girls make for all of the animals?

 Circle your answer.   0   1   2   3   4   5

How many earmuffs should the girls make for all of the animals?

 Circle your answer.   2   3   4   5   6   7

Diane's Pets

The girls had so much fun making clothes for Jada's pets that they decided to make clothes for Diane's pets. Diane has 2 dogs, 3 cats, and 4 lovebirds.

How many shoes should the girls make?

 Circle your answer.

20   22   24   26   28   30

How many hats should the girls make?

 Circle your answer.   1   2   3   4   5   6   7   8   9

How many earmuffs should the girls make?

 Circle your answer.   6   7   8   9   10   11   12   13   14

Family Matters!

Sally has 2 brothers and 3 sisters.

How many girls are in the family?

 Circle your answer.   1   2   3   4   5   6

How many children are in the family?

 Circle your answer.   1   2   3   4   5   6

How many hands do the children have altogether?

 Circle your answer.   10   12   15   18   20   22

How many fingers do the children have altogether?

 Circle your answer.   30   40   50   60   70

Balancing Act

For a scale to balance, there must be the same amount of weight on both ends. This scale has 10 on each end, so it is in balance.

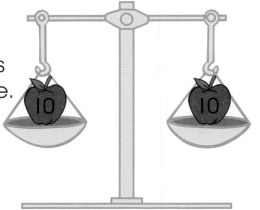

This scale is out of balance. It has 20 on the left end, but only 9 on the right end. How much should be put on the right end to make the scale balance?

 Circle your answer.   9   10   11   12   13   14

This scale is also out of balance. It has 30 on the right end, but only 18 on the left end. How much should be put on the left end to make the scale balance?

 Circle your answer.   10   12   20   21   30   31

Keeping Things in Balance

For a scale to balance, there must be the same amount of weight on both ends. This scale has 12 on each end, so it is in balance.

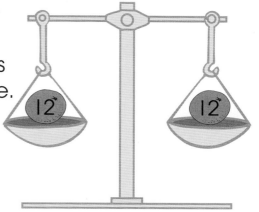

This scale is out of balance. It has 50 on the left end, but only 25 on the right end. How much should be put on the right end to make the scale balance?

 Circle your answer.   5   10   15   20   25   30

This scale is out of balance the other way. It has 100 on the right end, but only 89 on the left end. How much should be put on the left end to make the scale balance?

 Circle your answer.   11   21   19   29   31   39

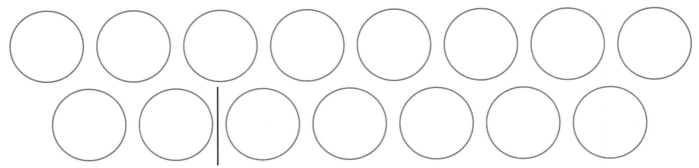

Going Around in Circles!

 Color 2 circles. Use different colors.
How many circles are **not** colored?

 Circle your answer.   10   11   12   13   14   15

 Color 3 more circles. Use different colors.
How many circles are colored now?

 Circle your answer.   5   6   7   8   9   10

How many circles are **not** colored?

 Circle your answer.   10   11   12   13   14   15

 Color half of the remaining circles.
How many circles are colored now?

 Circle your answer.   10   11   12   13   14   15

How many circles are **not** colored?

 Circle your answer.   5   6   7   8   9   10

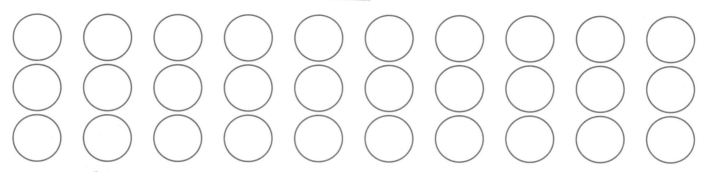
Going Around Again!

 Color 5 circles. Use different colors.
How many circles are **not** colored?

Circle your answer.   0   5   10   15   20   25

 Color 5 more circles. Use different colors.
How many circles are colored now?

Circle your answer.   0   5   10   15   20   25

How many circles are **not** colored?

Circle your answer.   0   5   10   15   20   25

 Color half of the remaining circles. Use different colors.
How many circles are colored now?

Circle your answer.   0   5   10   15   20   25

How many circles are **not** colored?

Circle your answer.   0   5   10   15   20   25

What Number Am I?

-5   0   5   10   15   20   25   30   35   40   45   50   55   60

I am a number that is bigger than 15 and smaller than 30. What number am I?

 Circle your answer.   44   12   9   29   14   31

I am a number that is bigger than 30 and smaller than 50. What numbers can I be?

 Circle your answers.   24   35   46   17   50   12

Look at the number line to help you answer this question: What number is in the middle between 0 and 30?

 Circle your answer.   0   5   10   15   20   25   30

Name _____

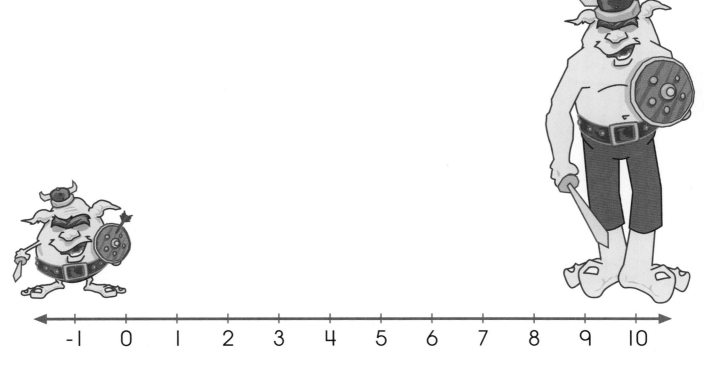

-1　0　1　2　3　4　5　6　7　8　9　10

I am a number that is bigger than 0 and smaller than 1. What number am I?

 Circle your answer.　0　$\frac{1}{2}$　1　$1\frac{1}{2}$　2　$2\frac{1}{2}$　3

I am a number that is bigger than 19. What numbers can I be?

 Circle your answer.　19　34　12　53　14　65

Look at the number line to help you answer this question: What number is in the middle between 0 and 7?

 Circle your answer.　2　$2\frac{1}{2}$　3　$3\frac{1}{2}$　4　$4\frac{1}{2}$　5

Cornering the Market

 Circle all the shapes that have corners.

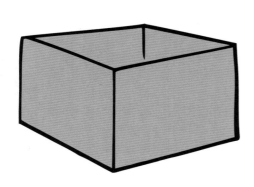

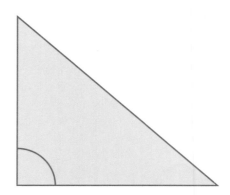

 Draw and color a shape that has at least 3 corners.

Round and Round

 Circle all the shapes that have rounded edges.

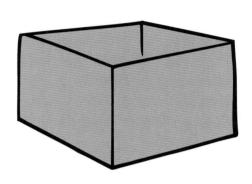

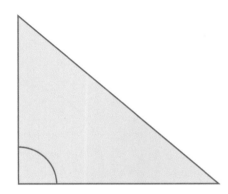

Draw and color a shape different from the ones above that has rounded edges.

Name _____

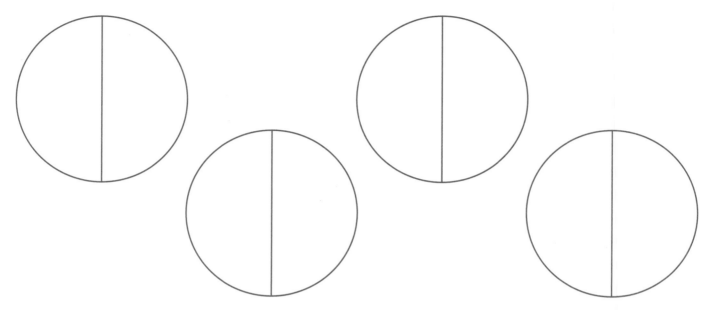

How many circles are there?

 Circle your answer.   1   2   3   4   5   6   7   8

 Color half of each circle a different color.
How many different colors did you use?

 Circle your answer.   1   2   3   4   5   6   7   8

If you had used 20 colors, how many circles would there be?

 Circle your answer.   3   4   5   6   7   8   9   10

If you had 15 circles to color, how many different colors would you need to use?

 Circle your answer.   15   18   20   23   27   30   33   35

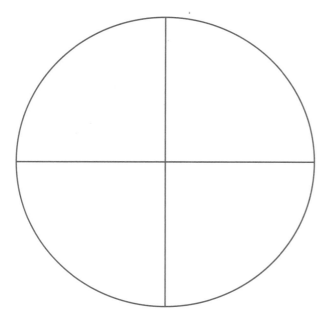 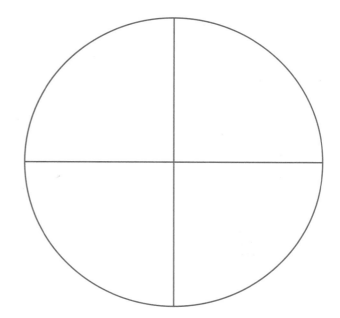

How many circles are there?

 Circle your answer.　　1　2　3　4　5　6　7　8

Color each part of the circles above a different color.
How many different colors did you use?

 Circle your answer.　　1　2　3　4　5　6　7　8

If you had 4 circles to color, how many different colors would you need to use?

 Circle your answer.　　15　16　17　18　19　20

If you had used 20 colors, how many circles would there be?

 Circle your answer.　　1　2　3　4　5　6　7　8

Name _____

The thermometer above shows the temperature as 10 degrees. Then the temperature falls 10 degrees.

What is the temperature now?

 Circle your answer.

-3   -2   -1   0   1   2   3

The thermometer on the right shows the temperature as 5 degrees. Then the temperature falls 5 degrees.

What is the temperature now?

 Circle your answer.

-3   -2   -1   0   1   2   3

Answer Key—Reading

Page 9
The monkey and bird are small. The elephant and leopard are large. The iguana and piranha are scaly. The monkey and bird are soft. Answers will vary.

Page 10
Pictures will vary, but Juniper should be between Jack and Jill in size.

Page 11
Children should circle the dragonfly, motor boat, frog.
Children should draw an X on the rowboat, snail, turtle, and ladybug.

Page 12
Answers will vary.
Children should draw a check mark on the hare.

Page 13

Page 14

Answers will vary.

Page 15

Pictures will vary.

Page 16
The two birds have feathers. The worm and the snakes have no legs. The horse would be fun to ride and so would possibly the elephant. The animal that is circled will vary.

Page 17

Answers will vary.

Page 18

Page 19

Page 20

Page 21

Page 22

Page 23

Page 24
Children should color the blanket and pillow, the box of Kleenex, the pillow, and the cat red. The quarter, log, and soccer ball should be colored appropriately.

Page 25
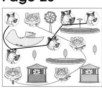

Page 26
Children should draw an **X** on the tennis racket in Row 1, the plate in Row 2, the TV in Row 3, and the skateboard in Row 4.

Page 27
Children should circle the hand, the finger, and thumb in Row 1; the cough syrup, the apple juice, and Kleenex in Row 2; the sun, moon, and stars in Row 3; and the shorts, t-shirt, and bathing suit in Row 4.

Page 28
Children should draw an **X** on the poodle, the cow, the shark, the zebra, the kangaroo, and the whale.

Page 29
Ladies' wigs, toilet bowl cleaner, and lawn chair do not belong.

Page 30
The girl's arms, the apple, the boy's teeth, the mouse, and the sandwiches should not be purple.

Page 31
Children should circle the banana in Row 1, the cowboy in Row 2, the computer in Row 3, and the bed in Row 4.

Page 32
Answers will vary.

Page 33

Page 34

Page 35

Page 36
Children's pictures will vary.

Page 37

Page 38

Page 39

Page 40

Page 41
Children should circle the football helmet in Row 1, the school bus in Row 2, the lime in Row 3, and the blueberries in Row 4.

Page 42
Children should circle the orange juice in Row 1, the ruler in Row 2, the dress in Row 3, and licorice in Row 4.

Page 43
Children should color the ice cream in Row 1, the basketball player 0 in Row 2, the tea kettle in Row 3, and the pig in Row 4.

Page 44
Children should color the sun in Row 1, the rabbit in Row 2, the porpoise in Row 3, and the elephant in the water in Row 4.

Page 45
Children should color the sun in Row 1, the ruler in Row 2, and the flower in Row 3.

Page 46

Page 47

Page 48
Children should draw a check mark by the third box.

Page 49
Children should draw a check mark by the second box.

Page 50
Children should draw a check mark by the first box.

Page 52
Children should draw and color the piece of candy with pink stripes.

Page 53
Children should draw a check mark on the second picture.

Page 54
Children should draw a check mark on the first picture.

Page 55
Children should draw a check mark on the last picture.

Page 56

Page 57
Children should draw an **X** on the battery, hammer, screwdriver, glass of water, flashlight, candy, and soap. Pictures will vary.

Page 58
Children should draw an **X** on the boot, bat, easel, jacket, and golf ball. Pictures will vary.

Page 59
Children should draw an **X** on the trumpet, the chocolate bar, the drum, and the TV. Pictures will vary.

Page 60
Children should draw an **X** on the saw, the jump rope, the rake, the airplane kit, the mitten, and the tree.

Page 61
Children should circle the first box.

Page 62
Children should circle the first box.

Page 63
Children should circle the first box.

Page 64
Children should circle the first box.

Page 65
Children should circle the second box.

Page 66
Children should circle the first box

Answer Key—Writing

Page 67

Page 68
Pictures for Dd, Gg, and Ll will vary.

Page 69
Pictures for Pp, Rr, and Uu will vary.

Page 70
Circle: Always, ask, Alice, after, any, ask

Page 71
Answers will vary. Circle: beaver, banana, bicycle, bunny, blanket, bear, ball, bird, bell, berries, bushes. Stories will vary.

Page 72
Pictures will vary.

Page 73
Circle: deer, Dalmatian, dog, dig, daisy, ducks

Page 74
Coloring of eggs will vary.

Page 75
Circle: fish, frog, fire, feather, fishing pole, fox
Sentences will vary.

Page 76
Circle: pig, flag, frog, bag, bug, log, wig, rug, zig zag. Sentences will vary.

Page 77
Circle: hairbrush, harp, hammer, ham, hat, hen, half-colored ball, half moon. Sentences will vary.

Page 79
Circle: lamp, lion, ladder

Page 80
Color red: mat, mug, moon, mailbox, map, man

Page 81
Draw: a napkin, name, nest, and needle

Page 82
Sentences will vary.

Page 83
Sentences and pictures will vary.

Page 84
Sentences and pictures will vary.

Page 85

Sentences will vary.

Page 86
Circle: sandwich, snail, sailboat, seal, sea horse, saw, snake, sun. Pictures will vary.

Page 87
Ideas of things that begin with Tt, Uu, and Vv will vary.

Page 88
Washcloth, window, wind, well, wing

Page 89
Sentences and pictures will vary.

Page 90
Color the Xx's blue, the Yy's red, and the Zz's green. Answers and pictures will vary.

Page 91

A		V
C		A
U		D
X		L
D		

Page 92
h, k l, N, Q R, t, V, Z; G, I, K, Q, S, W, Y; K, L, O, P, u, v

Page 93

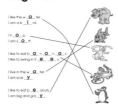

Page 94
Circle: pumpkin, pie, pig; towel, tie, tiger; bank, bowl, balloon; fly, fan, flower; deer, duck, doll. Pictures will vary.

Page 95

Page 96
Letters and designs will vary. Lists and pictures will vary.

Page 97

Page 98

Page 99

Page 100
Mug, pots, step, ten. Sentences will vary.

Page 101
Squirrel. Stories will vary.

Page 102
A table. t, a, b, l, e

Page 103l

p	o	u	t	c	u	t	e
i	l	z	h	m	o	v	e
c	s	p	a	c	k	a	w
k	t	u	n	b	h	f	o
s	o	c	k	g	d	v	q

Page 104
Children will copy words. Stories will vary.

Page 105
Children will copy words. Answers will vary.

Page 106
Sentences and answers will vary.

Page 107
A princess. Sentences will vary. Juggling. Sentences will vary. Answers will vary.

Page 108
Coyotes. Sentences will vary.

Page 109
I play tennis. My mom sings. Your dog howls. She likes to collect shells.

Page 110
Children will add periods at the end of each sentence.

Page 111
Sentences will vary. Capitalize Eddie, Max, and My.

Page 112
Sentences will vary. Capitalize July, Texas, April, Spain, Bob.

Page 113
Circle: dog food, leash, dog brush. Answers will vary.

Page 114
Pictures and words will vary. Stories will vary.

Page 115
Answers will vary.

Page 116
Circle: tablet, crayon, pencil, eraser. Pictures and words will vary.

Page 117

moon-spoon
punk-skunk
weird-beard
snake-cake

Page 118
Words and pictures will vary.

Page 119
Words and pictures will vary.

Page 120
Answers will vary.

Page 121
Answers will vary.

Page 122
Answers will vary.

Page 123
Pictures and stories will vary.

Page 124
Answers and pictures will vary.

Page 125
Answers and pictures will vary.

Answer Key—Math

Page 127

Page 128

Page 129
9 1
3 7
10 10
14 6

Page 130
8
12

Page 131

Page 132
9 1 2; 3 4 5
9 4 7; 8 7 5
10 15 5; 19 10 1
25 25 30 20; 20
30 30 20

Page 133
less than 2 minutes
3 minutes
less than 4 feet
8 inches

Page 134
9
40¢

Page 135
stars
2
moons
1
25

Page 136
12
5
4
3

Page 137
4
5
18

Page 138
20
6

Page 139
0
0

Page 140
5
0

Page 141

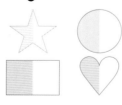

1 piece of 3

Page 142
6
shade 5 circles
5
shade 10 circles
10
shade $4\frac{1}{2}$ circles
$4\frac{1}{2}$

Page 143
16
8
3

Page 144
15
12

Page 146

Patterns will vary.

Page 147

Patterns will vary.

Page 148

Page 149

Page 150

Page 151

Page 152

Page 153

Page 154
Pictures of vertical
and horizontal
objects will vary.

Page 155
ounce
inch
quart

Page 156
scale
measuring cup
tape measurer

Page 157

Page 158

Pictures will vary.

Page 159

Page 160
years
inches
pounds

Page 161

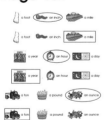

Page 162

Page 163

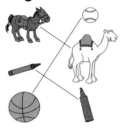

Page 164
neither are flat
one is square and
one is not
both are square
one is flat and one is
not

Page 165

Page 166

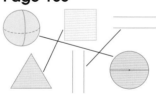

Pictures will vary.

Page 167
cars
dump trucks
1

Page 168
quarters
nickels
Bar graphs will vary.

Page 169
16
$6\frac{1}{2}$

Page 170
12
7

Page 171
14
4
4

Page 172
28
9
9

Page 173
4
6
12
60

Page 174
11
12

Page 175
25
11

Page 176
13
5
10
10
5

Page 177
25
10
20
20

10

Page 178
29
35, 46
15

Page 179
$\frac{1}{2}$
34, 53, 65
$3\frac{1}{2}$

Page 180

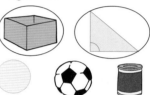

Shapes will vary.

Page 181

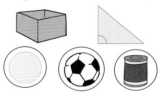

Shapes will vary.

Page 182
4
8
10
30

Page 183
2
8
16
5

Page 184
0
0

Notes